MW01248250

On This Night

Christmastime Devotions and Meditations

Marc E. Nauman

WESTBOW
P R E S S®
A DIVISION OF THOMAS NELSON
& ZONDERVAN

WestBow Press books may be ordered through booksellers or by contacting:

WestBow Press
A Division of Thomas Nelson & Zondervan
1663 Liberty Drive
Bloomington, IN 47403
www.westbowpress.com
844-714-3454

ISBN: 978-1-6642-5904-1 (sc)
ISBN: 978-1-6642-5903-4 (hc)
ISBN: 978-1-6642-5905-8 (e)

Library of Congress Control Number: 2022903487

Printed in the United States of America.

WestBow Press rev. date: 09/09/2022

Contents

Preface

Before you formed me in the womb, you knew me. Before I was born, you sanctified me and set me apart to be a spokesperson for you. And I said, "Ah, Lord, I can't do this!" (For too many reasons to enumerate!) And you said, "Don't say that!" I must go where you send me and speak what you give me and should not be afraid of their faces (or their reactions), for you are with me to deliver me. And then you reached out your hand and touched my lips and said, "Behold, I have put my words in your mouth" (Jeremiah 1:4–9, paraphrased).

This is my prayer before I preach, teach, write a sermon, or otherwise engage in any public speaking whatsoever. You'll notice, as I mention above, that this prayer is paraphrased from Jeremiah 1:4–9. Jeremiah was a reluctant prophet who overcame great fear and insecurities to follow God's call to be His spokesperson. As someone who fears public speaking, I can identify with the prophet Jeremiah! But over the years, I've learned that God's grace is mightier than my fears, and His love is greater than my insecurities. I often tell people that somewhere along my journey into ministry, the passion God gave me to share His Word overcame my fear and insecurities.

This Christmastime devotion is the first in a series of devotions entitled, "Your Words in My Mouth." In the following pages, you will find meditations and devotions centered around our Christmas Eve and Christmas Day celebrations at Trinity Lutheran Church, in Trinity, Florida. These are the words that God placed in my mouth to share with my congregation, you, and all of God's family. My hope is that you will be encouraged in the faith and that your heart will be filled with the joy of the Christ-child, born to us on the most blessed of nights. May His peace be with you.

Chapter 1

WHAT IS MISSING?

The year 2013 was exciting for Trinity Lutheran Church. In 2005, our congregation began worshipping in the cafeteria at Trinity College (no affiliation). After that, we held worship services in a double-wide modular for about five years. In April 2013, we finally were able to build our own brick-and-mortar facility. Although the sanctuary seated only about eighty people, we could not have been happier. Humble beginnings led to modest growth and great potential for the future.

But on this night, our focus was on the birth of our Savior. Our little sanctuary was decorated with four warmly lit Christmas wreaths that had been handcrafted by one of our longtime members. Two wreaths hung on each side wall. The ceiling lights were dimmed, which allowed the altar candles to burn brighter than ever. The lectern, from which the Christmas story would soon be recited and the homily delivered, received its light from those same altar candles. Our service began, and our hearts were filled with joyful anticipation as every seat was filled—except for one. I invite you to take that seat and listen in.

"What Is Missing?"—Christmas Eve, 2013

Luke 2:10–12 says, "And the angel said to them, 'Fear not, for behold, I bring you good news of a great joy that will be for all the people. For unto you is born this day in the city of David a Savior, who is Christ the Lord. And this will be a sign for you: you will find a baby wrapped in swaddling clothes and lying in a manger.'"

I love everything about Christmas: the lights, the celebrations, the families huddled around the Christmas tree early on Christmas morning, children's eyes all aglow with unbridled expectations! Like many of you, I have fond memories of my childhood Christmases, and in many ways, I want to capture those memories that I've cherished and relive them with my children. My hope is that they will do the same with their children. You see, that's the value of family traditions: sharing and continuing those things that we've come to cherish so deeply.

Christmas is one of those deeply cherished traditions, and if the places I've been to this Christmas season are any indication, millions of people still cherish their Christmas traditions. Millions of people continue to celebrate Christmas in some way, shape, or form. Their motives may sometimes be questionable, but they still acknowledge that there *is* something special about this time of year, something worth noticing, and that's a good thing! Even if it's only for a few hurried weeks at the end of the year, many people who would otherwise never give it a second thought will pause ever so briefly to consider the story of an angel who delivered a message of good news and of great joy: the story of a virgin who miraculously conceived and brought forth a son and how this little baby lying in a manger would be named Jesus.

There is no valid argument against the historical account that a baby named Jesus was born and lived, died on a cross, and that His tomb is still empty. In addition, there is no denying the significance of these events in human history. Now, whether you believe it, understand it, or even care about it, is an entirely different issue. There's also no denying that Christmas puts Jesus's story on display for all to hear.

But even with all that is good about the celebration of Christmas, for most people, something is still missing. Please hear me on this: it's not Jesus. Jesus is not missing from the celebration of Christmas. Jesus is talked about, debated over, and, for the most part, He is included in some way in the Christmas celebration. It's not the scriptures, either; the scriptures are not missing from the celebration of Christmas. They're included in the hymns and songs that are sung and in the stories that are told and retold every year. I once went to SeaWorld in the beginning of December, and they were playing

Third Day's Christmas album throughout the park. The Christmas story, Jesus, and the scriptures were proclaimed for all to hear! But something was still missing.

There is a present sitting on the altar. It is beautifully wrapped—obviously, my wife wrapped it—and it even includes batteries (to avert a disaster with the kids tomorrow morning). But something is missing. What is it? You'll notice that there is no name tag on this gift. Who is it for? How do we know who to give it to? I could open it, but I'm not sure if it's for me. There's nothing worse than opening a gift that is not for you! So, without a name tag, I'd better set it aside until we can figure out who it is for. We can admire this gift and talk about how beautiful it is, but we dare not open it.

Understand that this is what is missing when most people celebrate Christmas. Christmas is not just *about* Christ. The Christmas story, the gospel, is not just *about* Christ. As Luther said, "Christ has given himself *for*

5

you."[1] The gospel isn't the gospel until it is Christ *for you.* The gospel is more than just an abstract construct for philosophers to discuss. The Christmas story is more than just a retelling of events for historians to speculate over. Christmas is the direct intervention of a very real God into human history for very real people—way back then, and even today. Christmas is Christ *for you* and *for me.*

Think about the scriptures for a moment. The prophets didn't predict that a child would be born or that a son would be given. They said, "For to us a child is born, to us a son is given" (Isaiah 9:6). The angels didn't announce that a Savior was born. They said, "For unto you is born this day in the city of David a Savior, who is Christ the Lord" (Luke 2:11). Mary didn't praise Almighty God for the great things He had done but rather, she praised, "He who is mighty who has done great things for me" (Luke 1:49). The baby who slept in

---

[1] Martin Luther, "A Brief Instruction on What to Look for and Expect in the Gospels," *Luther's Works,* eds. E. Theodore Bachmann and Helmut T. Lehmann, vol. 35 (Philadelphia: Fortress Press, 1971), 120.

the manger wasn't just God; He was Emmanuel, God *with us.* Jesus has come to save us from our sins. Our sins are real; our need for forgiveness is real; and God chose to save us through a real, historical act of intervention. We must understand that Christmas is just as much the activity of God today as it was two thousand years ago. For two thousand years and running, Christmas has continuously proclaimed that Jesus has come for you and for me, that we can be forgiven of our sins, and that we receive His gift of salvation and eternal life.

As we celebrate Christmas this evening and tomorrow, I hope all the presents under your tree have name tags on them. But more importantly, I hope you believe that the Christmas story has your name tag on it! It's addressed from God *to you.* A Savior has come for you. He is Christ the Lord! Will you bow your heads and pray with me?

Our gracious, heavenly Father, hallow this night so that it may be your holy night for us. Help us hear your Spirit speaking through your Word so that we may no longer live in darkness. Lead us to listen to the gospel, your good news, so that we may know your Son born to us—our Savior, Christ, our Lord. Open our hearts to hear the mighty choirs sing of your promises so that we may see your glory in Christ's humble birth. May His peace be for us. Let Him who once was born be born anew in our hearts this blessed night. Amen.

Chapter 2

GOD'S TREASURE

"Christmas comes softly, silently, sweetly, wrapping
its loveliness about the world … and once again
the most beautiful message on earth is repeated …
peace on earth, good will toward men."
—Helen Steiner Rice

Many years ago, I received a Christmas card with a bookmark attached to the inside cover. Printed on the bookmark was the above quote from the late Helen Steiner Rice, an American writer of religious and inspirational poetry. Over time, what seemed to be a simple gift from a friend has become a treasure. For over thirty years now, I've been using this same bookmark in my Bibles, seminary books, Greek lectionaries, and so forth. I guess you could call me sentimental, but every time I read the words on this bookmark, they draw me in and remind me of the beauty of the Christmas message. God loves us so much that He gave *Himself* to us in His Son, to forgive us of our sins and make us His children once again.

A bookmark is a simple treasure, but then again, aren't most treasures? It's the simple things in life that become our greatest treasures. Once again, I invite you to listen in to another Christmas Eve meditation at Trinity Lutheran Church and discover what God treasures this Christmas season.

"God's Treasure"—Christmas Eve, 2015

In our gospel reading from Luke 2:17–19, Luke writes that the shepherds "made known the saying that had been told them concerning this child. And all who heard it wondered at what the shepherds told them. But Mary treasured up all these things, pondering them in her heart."

I love the last part of that passage: "But Mary treasured up all these things." When it comes to Christmas, there are a lot of things to treasure up. Christmas is a great time of the year, and we all have things that we treasure during this season, including our traditions, our families, and our friends. What about the gifts? Oh, yeah! We make a list of all the things we treasure, and we give them to our spouses or maybe to our parents. These are all the things that we treasure this Christmas. And if we're being honest, this becomes the focal point during Christmas season—not only the curiosity of what I am going to get for Christmas, but also what I am going to give to my wife, my kids, and my friends. The desire to find just the right gift is important to us. It matters immensely. Look at the malls, the outlet stores, and the online traffic; the stores are packed and busier than ever! That's just a reflection of how busy we are, shopping for *just the right thing*, because things are important to us.

This reminds me of a lecture I heard from a professor when I was in seminary. He said that throughout history, humankind has always been more concerned with *having* rather than with *being*. We're more concerned with what we possess than with who we are. I would have to agree with him. Look at our Christmas lists: did anyone ask to be a nicer person or to be kinder and more patient? Did anyone ask to be a more forgiving person or to be less selfish? Probably not. (I know I didn't!) We are more concerned with having rather than with being, and we've been that way for a long time. Even in Jesus's day, many folks followed Jesus only because of what they could get from Him: free food, physical healing, and even free wine on occasion. I believe there is a good reason why humankind has always been more concerned with having rather than with being.

You see, no matter how hard we try, we have never been able to change who we are. And it's not for lack of trying! We've all made New Year's resolutions that we almost never keep. We've recommitted ourselves to something important to us only to fall away time and time again. Therefore, when faced with the sobering reality of who we really are, there's only one thing left for us to do: we go shopping! That's one thing we can do, and it masks our real dilemmas, at least for a little while. But at the end of the day when we look in the mirror, the sobering reality hits us once again: we can't change who we are.

The apostle Paul struggled with this same dilemma. In Romans 7:15–24, Paul writes, "I don't understand my own actions ... I have the desire to do what is right, but not the ability to carry it out. I do not do the good I want, but the evil I do not want is what I keep on doing ... Wretched man that I am! Who will deliver me from this body of death?" I know who: Macy's! They're having a great sale. Or Publix. They have all those buy-one, get-one-free items on sale. Boy, do they make me feel good. Obviously, that isn't the answer Paul gives us.

No matter what we have and no matter how many things we accumulate, it will never change who we are. "Wretched man that I am! Who will deliver me?" Paul then says, "Thanks be to God through Jesus Christ our Lord!" (Romans 7:25). As wretched people, we have the tendency to treasure all the wrong things, but do you know what God treasures this Christmas? He treasures you. He treasures you so much that He does something for you that you could never do for yourself: He transforms who you are. In the Bible, God reveals how your transformation takes place.

God transforms you and me as we hear His Word. Hebrews 4:12 says, "For the word of God is living and active, sharper than any two-edged sword, piercing to the division of soul and of spirit, of joints and of marrow, and discerning the thoughts and intentions of the heart." God speaks the same Word that created heaven and earth over you and me in our baptisms, in the sermon, and in the hymns we sing. God speaks His Word and brings to life a new creation *in us*. The old has passed away; behold, the new has come. You may be thinking to yourself, *What does this have to do with Christmas?*

Let me answer that by asking you a question: Who is Jesus? Jesus is God's Word made flesh, and a little later in the service, you'll hear this truth in the gospel of incarnation in John 1:1–14. Jesus is the very essence of God's Word in human flesh. Realize that the baby wrapped in swaddling clothes and lying in the manger is not just the reason for the season. Jesus is the only reason we can be transformed into who God created us to be. And God so loved you and me that He gave His only begotten Son. God gave Jesus to us, not so we could acquire more things, but so we could become His children! The scripture 1 John 3:1–2 says, "See what kind of love the Father has given to us that we should be called children of God; and so we are." What a gift from God! God has given us the gift of being His children through faith in His only Son, Jesus Christ, the Word made flesh.

Let's venture back to our opening verse from Luke: "But Mary treasured up all these things" (Luke 2:19). What things did Mary treasure up? Did she treasure up the gifts of gold, frankincense, and myrrh that the wise men brought? No. They hadn't arrived yet. Did she treasure up the buy-one, get-one deal from Publix? No. Publix hadn't quite expanded into that region of the world yet. Mary treasured up "the saying that had been told them concerning this child" (Luke 2:17). She treasured up God's Word, and on that night, some two thousand years ago, "The Word became flesh and dwelt among us" (John 1:14). Tonight, He dwells among us once again.

Chapter 3

WRAPPED

By now, you've probably realized that the Christmas season at Trinity Lutheran Church is a special time. As a congregation, we like to reach out to our community and share the Christmas Spirit in a variety of ways. One of our favorite ways is through our senior wish tree. Every year, church members select envelopes from the wish tree that contain the names and gift requests of homebound senior citizens in our community. They don't have the means to go Christmas shopping, so we do our best to provide what they've asked for on their Christmas lists. Another way we share the Christmas spirit is by inviting the community to join us for our annual Christmas cookie celebration sponsored by our youth group and most recently by our ladies' guild. Anything involving food—especially cookies—is always a good way to bring the community together.

However, there was an outreach event that wasn't as successful as we had hoped. We thought that providing free gift wrapping to our neighbors was a great way to share the Christmas spirit. It's not that this was necessarily a bad idea; it's just that most people, at least in our experience, bought many of their presents at the last minute and ended up wrapping the gifts themselves on Christmas Eve. As a result, we had many volunteers who wrapped only one or two gifts during their four-hour shifts in the weeks leading up to Christmas. Needless to say, our gift wrapping efforts lasted only one year. But this didn't dampen our Christmas spirits. We were back at it the next year, baking delicious Christmas cookies and drawing names from our senior wish tree.

"Wrapped"—Christmas Eve, 2018

There are a lot of great things to do during the Christmas season: parties, Christmas cantatas, shopping, opening gifts, spending time with family and friends, going to Christmas Town at Busch Gardens, and even coming to church! Did I miss anything? You'll notice that I didn't mention wrapping gifts. Of all the great things to do during the Christmas season, wrapping gifts probably doesn't rank all that high. It's more like something we *have* to do. My wife and I used to wait until Christmas Eve to wrap gifts; that was our tradition. But after our second child was born (we now have four), we didn't have the time or energy to wrap all those gifts on Christmas Eve anymore! Even worse, sometimes to avoid wrapping a gift, we'd just put it in a gift bag. If you think about it, gift bags are an odd thing to use. You pay fifty times more for a gift bag than for wrapping paper just so you don't have to wrap a gift!

Gift wrapping is also odd. I don't know about you, but I look for the cheapest wrapping paper possible.

After all the pomp and ceremony is over, the paper just ends up in the garbage can. I remember on one occasion when my daughter and I were Christmas shopping, and we needed some wrapping paper. She wanted to buy the fancy plaid paper because it looked classy. But there I was, comparing the price per square foot to get the best deal possible. I dare not overspend on wrapping paper! Now, picture this: We take the cheapest paper possible and wrap the most expensive gifts that we'll buy the entire year in it. Isn't that kind of odd? We wrap some of the most expensive gifts (jewelry, cell phones, a PS4) in the least expensive paper we can find. The wrapping paper does not befit or accurately represent the gift that lies hidden inside of it. However, there are a few precedents for doing this.

Think about human beings, for instance. When God created humans, He formed our bodies from the dust of the ground. Genesis 2:7–8 says, "The Lord God formed the man of dust from the ground and breathed into his nostrils the breath of life, and the man became a living creature." God took a pile of dirt (talk about some cheap wrapping paper) and breathed His precious gift of life into it, and we became living creatures. I'm not saying our physical bodies are worthless and don't matter. The Bible says, "We are fearfully and wonderfully made" (Psalm 139:14). But right now, because of sin and its effect on creation, our bodies are falling apart, imperfect, and flawed. Listen to the apostle Paul in 2 Corinthians 5:2–5: "For while we're in this tent we groan, longing to put on our heavenly dwelling …"

While we're in this physical wrapping paper, we long for something more. I think you all would agree, it's what's on the inside that makes us valuable and makes us who we are. How many different sayings do we have to that affect? "You can't judge a book by its cover. Appearances can be deceiving. It's what's on the inside that counts." God places His precious gift of life, and all that life entails, inside this wrapping paper. In its current state, humanity is one precedent. But there is another precedent for wrapping something precious in something common and inexpensive: it's what we celebrate at Christmas and why we're gathered here for worship.

When the eternal Son of God was born of a virgin, God literally wrapped himself in human flesh. You talk about a contrast! Listen to John 1:1–4, 14 (Note: this is a portion of the gospel of incarnation): "In the beginning was the Word, and the Word was with God, and the Word was God. He was in the beginning with God. All things were made through Him, and without Him was not anything made. In Him was life itself, and the life was the light of men … And the Word became flesh and dwelt among us, and we have seen His glory, glory as of the only Son from the Father, full of grace and truth." Jesus is God wrapped in our flesh. Can we even understand what that means? Luther didn't think so. He said, "Human reason does not apprehend it and should turn utterly blind, dark and foolish and step out of its old false light into a new light."[2]

Hear me on this: the very essence of God, the same

---

[2] Martin Luther, *Weimar Ausgabe* (Weimar, Germany: Hermann Bohlau, 1889), vol. 10, 239.

God who formed humanity out of the dust from the ground and breathed life into us, the same God who made all things and who spoke in the desert at Mt. Sinai to the children of Israel and parted the Red Sea, the same God who rained manna from heaven, the one true God, the essence of life itself and everything we know about our existence—this same God wrapped Himself in our flesh. Luther continued, "All the majesty of God was masked and wrapped in Jesus' humanity. God has hidden His majesty in Christ. He does not appear with lightning, thunder, or angels, but as one born of a virgin and speaking with men about the forgiveness of sins."[3]

God wrapped Himself in our flesh so that we could see Him, hear Him, touch Him, and know Him. Apart from Jesus, it is not possible for us to see the majesty of God. But God wants to be seen, heard, touched, and known. Therefore, He wrapped Himself in human flesh and was born of a virgin. What a gift! In Jesus, the fullness of the Godhead dwells in bodily form. As the

---

[3] Martin Luther, *Weimar Ausgabe* (Weimar, Germany: Hermann Bohlau, 1889), vol. 47, 209.

apostle Paul says in Philippians 2:6–8, "He was in the form of God ... but made himself nothing, taking the form of a servant, being born in the likeness of men. And being found in human form, he humbled himself by becoming obedient to the point of death, even death on a cross." What did humanity do with that gift? We did what we do with every gift: We tore it open and ripped it apart! But on the cross, God unwrapped the greatest gift of all time. For God so loved His creation that He gave Himself to us through His only Son, that whosoever believes in Him would not perish in their sins but have everlasting life! Life itself was wrapped in Jesus's humanity, and that gift of life was unwrapped on the cross. The majesty of God is hidden beneath human flesh, and we partake of His majesty through faith in Jesus.

Through faith in Jesus, we're forgiven of our sins and have eternal life. That means we have eternal life right now! It may not seem like it, and it may not feel like it, which is why Paul says in 2 Corinthians 4:7–8, "We have this treasure in jars of clay to show that the surpassing power belongs to God and not to us." That brings us full circle, back to the first precedent. As human creatures in this life and in these bodies, we share in Christ's sufferings, but we will reign with Him and share in His majesty in the life to come. So, this Christmas, as you're tearing open your presents, pause for a moment, think about Jesus, and thank God for the greatest gift ever unwrapped! Amen.

Chapter 4

THE GIFT OF LIFE

Like Christmas at Trinity, Advent is also a special time of the year. During the four weeks of Advent, the excitement and anticipation of celebrating Christ's birth crescendos into our Christmas Eve celebration. However, as exciting as it can be, Advent presents somewhat of a challenge for many pastors. Every year at our November get-togethers, we ask each other, "What are you doing for Advent this year?" Over the years, I've experimented with various services and activities that emphasize the meaning of Advent for my congregation. We've tried everything from traditional Advent services to service projects, such as caroling at nearby assisted living facilities.

One of my favorite Advent celebrations was focused

on Dietrich Bonhoeffer's *God Is in the Manger: Reflection on Advent and Christmas.* The services were intimate, candle-lit, and devotional in style. We sang hymns and a cappella carols and discussed various portions of Bonhoeffer's work. Without giving too much away (I highly recommend reading *God is in the Manger*), Bonhoeffer left a lasting impression on our celebration of Advent. We only wished that his life hadn't been cut so short. Making the most of the gift of life that God has given to each one of us, as Bonhoeffer did, is both a goal and an ongoing passion inspired by Bonhoeffer's life and witness.

"The Gift of Life"—Christmas Eve, 2017

What's the best thing about Christmas? The gifts! Most of the time, we give someone a gift because we love him or her and want to give the person something he or she needs. How many times during the Christmas season do we ask our loved ones, "What do you want or need for Christmas?" What I need and what I want are two different things! I need underwear and socks, but I want video games and electronic gadgets. We make every effort to give the right gifts to those we love, and we go to extreme measures to find out just what they need. But there are times when we just don't know what to give someone for Christmas. What do you give the person who doesn't need anything? Fortunately, God doesn't face that same dilemma when it comes to giving His gifts to us. God knows exactly what we need, and He knows exactly what we can't provide for ourselves.

Listen to this well-known verse, which, by the way, is a great verse for Christmas: "For God so loved the world, that He gave his only Son, that whoever believes in Him should not perish but have eternal life" (John 3:16). Why did God give us His only Son? Because He loves us! We were perishing under the weight of our sins, and God did something about it. Romans 6:23 reminds us, "For the wages of sin is death, but the gift of God is eternal life in Christ Jesus our Lord." God loves you so much that He gave Jesus to you so that, through believing in Him, you would not perish in your sins but have eternal life.

I told you, *the gifts* are the best thing about Christmas. You thought I was kidding! Let's consider one of those gifts: the gift of eternal life. Remember, according to scripture, we were created for eternity. We were created to live forever. We had eternity woven into the fiber of our beings, but we lost it. When Adam fell into sin, all humanity fell with him. "And the wages of sin is death" (Romans 6:23). We lost eternal life with God. Consequently, in our hearts there is a deep-seated, unfulfilled longing for something more. I would argue that this same longing is in the heart of every single human: a longing for eternity. In our hearts, we long for what we were supposed to be: eternal and timeless. This longing shows up in a variety of different ways at different times.

Christmastime is one example. I remember when we used to shop for our kids during the Christmas season. We would go to Toys-R-Us and, of course, the toy sections at Walmart and Target. We looked for the latest action figures, Pokémon, Barbie dolls, stuffed animals, and more. But my kids are older now; they're teenagers and young adults. We don't shop in the toy section anymore. When I've passed by the toy section in the last few years, I've realized my kids are growing up. I've also realized that we don't have all the time in the world. We have a limited amount of time to be together, and then they're grown. So, as I approach another Christmas, there is a certain amount of apprehension: joy and sorrow mingled together.

I like how Dietrich Bonhoeffer described it. He said, "We all come with different personal feelings to the Christmas festival. One comes with pure joy [the kids!]. Others come looking for a moment of peace [the parents!]. Yet others come with great apprehension and sorrow. Those who have lost loved ones or have no one to celebrate Christmas with [the elderly]."[4] Here's the kicker: I believe all these different feelings and longings are really one and the same. Whether it's a longing to go back to the way things used to be when life was better or a longing for time to stand still—or at least to slow down

---

[4] Dietrich Bonhoeffer, *God is in the Manger: Reflections on Advent and Christmas* (Westminster: John Knox Press, 2010), 55.

a little bit so we can catch our breath—it's all the same. Maybe we long to be with and to celebrate Christmas with those whom we love. Whatever the longing may be, it's all the same: it's a longing for eternal life, a longing for timelessness. Here's the real kicker: this longing, with all its joy, sorrow, and apprehension, comes from God. Ecclesiastes 3:11 says, "God has set eternity in the hearts of men; yet they cannot fathom it; what God has done from beginning to end ..." In our hearts, God places a longing for what we were supposed to be: timeless. But we can't fathom it.

Just for a moment, I want you to think about the Christmas scenarios I just shared with you. Imagine if time was no longer an issue. There would be no apprehension over our children growing older or of not having enough time together. We would have forever. There would be no sorrow over not being with the ones we love. We would have forever—no sorrow, pain, sin, or death. That is the gift of eternal life! Make no mistake about it: God has set a longing for eternity in the hearts of humankind to draw us to the source and giver of eternal life, His only Son, Jesus Christ.

In John 10:10, Jesus said, "I came that they may have life and have it abundantly." Apart from Jesus, there is no life; there is only death. "For the wages of sin is death, but the gift of God is eternal life in Christ Jesus our Lord" (Romans 6:23). Death makes time our enemy. Time is never on our side. Time may be a great teacher, but it's a terrible beautician. (So is gravity!) Apart from Jesus, we all run out of time. But God so loved the world that He gave His only Son that whoever believes in Him should not perish but have eternal life. Jesus said that! Jesus also said in John 11:25–26, "I am the resurrection and the life. Whoever believes in me, though he die, yet shall he live, and everyone who lives and believes in me shall never die." And then, Jesus simply asked this question: "Do you believe this?" Do you believe it? Do you believe what Jesus said? It's just that simple, believe Jesus.

On this Christmas Eve, as you approach another Christmas, whatever feelings you may be experiencing—joy, apprehension, sorrow—God has placed that longing within your heart to lead you to the manger and to lead you to Jesus. He knows exactly what you need. That's why Jesus was born in a manger, died on the cross, and rose from the dead for you, so that you can be forgiven of your sins and have eternal life through faith in Him. That is the gift God gave to us on the first Christmas and every Christmas thereafter. Like I said, the gifts are the best thing about Christmas! And may it be unto us according to your Word. Amen.

Chapter 5

SILENT NIGHT

One of our longstanding traditions at Trinity Lutheran Church is reading our monthly memory verses together as a congregation. Each month we have a different scripture to memorize. The verse is printed in the bulletin and recited together at the beginning of our worship services. I thoroughly enjoy both choosing the verses and attempting to memorize them. However, this tradition did not originate with me; rather, it was passed down to me from the founding pastor of Trinity, Rev. David Hammer.

Isn't that true of everything? Technically, we're not the originators of anything. Everything in our lives is passed down to us from someone else. On several occasions, I've reminded my parishioners that if they like my sermons, then they should thank my professors at seminary, my teachers at Bible college, the pastors who shepherded me along my Christian journey, and so on. I'm simply a mouthpiece for what has been passed down to me. Behind this pulpit stands a long line of people that stretches over the centuries: from my professors to their professors before them, all the way back to the apostles and to Jesus Christ Himself. I'm simply *their* mouthpiece, sharing the words God has given me from the lips (and the pens) of my brothers and sisters in Christ throughout the ages. Once again, I would be honored for you to lean in and listen to their words in a message I presented on Christmas Eve in 2016.

"Silent Night"—Christmas Eve, 2016

Our memory verse for the month of December was Hebrews 1:1–2. "Long ago, at many times and in many ways, God spoke to our fathers by the prophets, but in these last days he has spoken to us by his Son." I think this is another fantastic verse for Christmas! In these last days, God has spoken to us by His Son, Jesus Christ. If you think about the Christmas season, there's a lot of speaking going on! It's a noisy time of year: Christmas parties, Christmas music, Christmas shopping, and Christmas traffic! Last week, Christene and I went to the mall to do some shopping and to help Santa out a little bit—but the traffic! I've never heard so many car horns blaring at one time in my life. I thought maybe someone had that bumper sticker that says, "Honk if you love Jesus." We humans are noisy creatures, and even more so at Christmas.

Luther made a very astute observation about human beings. He believed that what makes us human is not our ability to reason, our will, or even our ability to love. What makes us human is our need to have faith. Luther insisted that the human heart is not made for itself; it's made to go outside itself and cling to that which speaks to the heart. Humans are hearing creatures whose hearts are always clinging to some word or another to find faith.[5] Faith requires something to hear. Romans 10:17 says, "Faith comes from hearing and hearing through the words of Christ." Our hearts receive faith from whatever word we're listening to or hanging on to. The words that we hear are the source of our faith; this is where our faith comes from.

As you are aware, there are a lot of different words floating around out there. You have politicians, lobbyists, and the internet (just google it! Ask Siri!). You have the media: FOX News, CNN, MSNBC, ESPN—so many different words to listen to, and all of them playing tug-of-war with our ears and vying for our heart's attention. How do we hear God's voice in the middle of all that noise? Where do we find *His words*? Some of us might think that to hear God's voice, we need to turn down or turn off all the outside noise and then listen to our inner voices, those still, small voices within. I don't know about you, but one of the noisiest places in the world is inside my own head! *I'm not crazy, either!* There are

---

[5] Steven D. Paulson, *Lutheran Theology* (London: Bloomsbury Academic, 2012), 56.

others who would argue that God doesn't really speak to us anymore and that in our day and age, God is more or less silent. They believe He has left it up to us to rely on our vast intellect to figure things out the best we can. But if that is the case, then it's not working out so well, is it?

So, does God speak to us—and if so, how? Let's get back to Hebrews 1: "Long ago, at many times and in many ways, God spoke to our fathers by the prophets, but in these last days He has spoken to us by His Son" (Hebrews 1:1–2). This is the Christmas story. This is the reason for the season. Right in the middle of all our noise, right in the middle of all those voices, God spoke and continues to speak to us. God is not silent. The *silent* in "Silent Night" is meant for us. Be still and know that He is God. God is not silent. If anything, God is a chatterbox! God spoke and keeps speaking throughout history through His Son. At Christmastime, God is as loud as ever.

The question is, "If God is so loud, then why don't we hear Him speaking?" Let me offer this advice: there's nothing more effective at drowning out the voice of God than when we listen to our own inner voices and think that they are God speaking to us. We make the mistake of confusing our internal voices with the voice of God, and we end up putting *our* words in *His* mouth. Understand, our inner voices (i.e., our voices of conscience or voices of reason) are not equivalent to—neither are they the same thing as—the voice of God or the voice of the Holy Spirit. Make no mistake about it: first and foremost, God's voice is an external voice. It comes from outside of us! On that blessed Christmas, God's Son took on flesh and was born in a manger. Jesus lived and dwelled among us, but He came to us from outside of us. He came from heaven. In John 1:1–14, the apostle John wrote, "In the beginning was the Word, and the Word was with God, and the Word was God … and the Word became flesh and dwelt among us." And at the Transfiguration, God, the Father, said, "This is my beloved Son with whom I am well pleased, listen to Him!" (Matthew 17:5). Jesus, the Word made flesh, is the only way that we can listen to God's voice. Jesus is the only way that we can know who God is and know God's love for us. And here's the thing: there is only one way for you and me to know for certain that we're listening to Jesus.

In John's gospel, Jesus said, "Blessed are those who have not seen and yet have believed" (John 20:29). John then writes, "Jesus did many other signs in the presence of the disciples, which are not written in this book: but these are written so that you may believe that Jesus is the Christ, the Son of God, and that by believing you may have life in his name" (John 20:30–31). The Word of Christ was written down for us and recorded in the pages of the Bible, so that we, too, can listen to Him and receive faith from hearing His Word. And every Christmas, His Word is preached from this pulpit and from hundreds of thousands of other pulpits around the world! Through pastors, preachers, and priests, God proclaims with a loud voice, "This is My Son. Listen to Him!" He died for you. He rose again from the dead for you so that you can be forgiven of your sins and receive eternal life. This is the Word our hearts need to listen to this Christmas. This is why Christ instituted His church, and this is why Christ calls people to preach the gospel—so His external voice can still be heard and our hearts can grab ahold of His Word. The heart is not made for itself; it's made to go outside itself and cling to that which speaks to the heart. Let me be clear, I'm not saying that God doesn't speak to our hearts or that the Holy Spirit doesn't guide us all the time. What I am saying is that the only way to be sure the inner voice we are hearing is God's voice is to test it with the scriptures. The Holy Spirit always points our hearts to Christ and His Word.

I conclude with what Dietrich Bonhoeffer said about God speaking to us through an external voice. Bonhoeffer said, "God has willed that we should hear His Living Word in the witness of a brother, in the mouth of a man. Therefore, the Christian needs another Christian who speaks God's Word to him … the Christ in his own heart is weaker than the Christ in the Word of his brother."[6] I pray that on this holy night, you've heard Christ's Word through the mouth of this weak brother, and I pray that in your heart, faith has been born anew and that you believe Jesus. That is the reason for the season. That is the Christmas story. And may it be unto us according to your Word, oh Lord. Amen.

---

[6] Dietrich Bonhoeffer, *Life Together* (Munich: Christian Kaiser Verlag, 1954), 23.

Chapter 6

UNEXPECTED

At the introduction to this book, I shared a prayer with you that is based on the first chapter of Jeremiah. I have another prayer to share with you; I call it my abbreviated prayer, although it's just as long as the Jeremiah prayer. I pray this one quite often, usually before I engage in speaking (and right after I pray the Jeremiah passage; the two prayers somewhat fit together). I also pray this when I'm feeling anxious, stressed out, or unsure about what the day ahead may hold. This is a great prayer for when I have no idea what to expect! It is also based on scripture passages that have been a source of strength and encouragement over the years. I placed those passages in parentheses beside the corresponding petitions. Here is the prayer:

"Your Words in my mouth (Jeremiah 1:9), Your Spirit in my heart (Galatians 4:6), Your strength in my weakness, Your glory in my suffering, (2 Corinthians 12:8–10). Help me to be conscious of you, conscious of the people I'm serving, and not to be self-conscious. Fill me with your Holy Spirit equal to the task at hand. Everything I face today you've prepared beforehand for me to walk in it. Help me to walk in it through faith in you (Ephesians 2:10). Power, passion, pause, boldness, confidence, and energy, in Jesus's name. Amen."

As usual, I prayed this prayer right before I stood behind the pulpit to deliver the following sermon.

"Unexpected"—Christmas Eve, 2019

In about twelve hours or so, our kids will be waking my wife and me to open presents. It's very exciting and very early, although it's not as early as it used to be. As my kids are getting older, they're learning the value of a good night's sleep. And when tomorrow morning finally arrives, under our tree will be an assortment of gifts waiting to be opened—some of which the kids asked for, and some of which Mom and Dad asked for. We all made our lists, and we gave them to the appropriate person (my wife), and then off she went to the North Pole to lend Santa a helping hand. But of all the gifts that will be under the tree, the most special are the *unexpected ones*—the gifts that weren't on anyone's list. Those are the best gifts of all.

Our text for this evening's meditation is found in Luke 2:4–7. "Joseph went up from the town of Nazareth to Bethlehem, the town of David, because he belonged to the house and line of David. He went there to register for the census with Mary, who was pledged to be married to him and was expecting a child. While they were there, the time came for the baby to be born, and she gave birth to her firstborn, a son. She wrapped him in cloths and placed him in a manger, because there was no room for them in the inn."

That first Christmas was all about an unexpected

gift: the birth of Christ the Lord. Think about Mary, when the angel first announced to her that she would conceive in her womb and bear a son and name Him Jesus. Mary was like "What? No way! How will this be?" The angel answered her. "The Holy Spirit will come upon you, and the power of the Most High will overshadow you; therefore, the child to be born will be called holy—the Son of God" (Luke 1:35). Think about Joseph. When he saw that Mary was pregnant, he resolved to divorce her quietly. This was certainly not what Joseph was expecting. "But then an angel of the Lord appeared to him in a dream, saying, "Joseph, do not be afraid to take Mary as your wife, for that which is conceived in her is from the Holy Spirit. She will bear a son, and you shall call his name Jesus, he will save his people from their sins" (Matthew 1:20–21).

And now, think about the little town of Bethlehem. Except for an inn keeper and few lowly shepherds, Bethlehem was asleep. They weren't expecting anything; it was just another night. What happened on that night, anyway? A baby was born in a manger. A baby was born in a trough used to feed animals. On that night, there were certainly more newsworthy events than this! There were certainly babies born in greater places: in Rome, in Antioch, or in Damascus. There were babies born in kings' palaces! However, in the vastness of all creation, God chose the most unexpected of places, Bethlehem, to announce that a Savior was born. And while this little town of Bethlehem was asleep, God, the Son, robed Himself in our flesh and was born in the most unexpected of ways. According to human standards, it was quite uneventful. There was no halftime show while Mary was in labor. There was no television coverage, no around-the-clock updates for the world to take note of. But isn't that the way God works? God chooses what is weak in this world to shame the strong. God chooses what is despised in this world so that no one can boast in His presence. On the night when Christ was born, for the most part, His own people didn't even know it. A tiny baby born in a manger in the most insignificant of cities is Christ, our Savior! He wasn't born a superhero; he wasn't Captain America or Superman. He was God, the Son, wrapped in the weakness and frailty of our flesh. A tiny little baby, helpless as any other, completely unexpected by almost everyone.

Let me point out that Jesus's earthly mission, His earthly ministry, didn't begin when He was baptized or when He was tempted in the wilderness. It didn't begin when He proclaimed the good news to the poor or when He healed the sick. It didn't begin when He was crucified or at His resurrection. It didn't even begin when He was born in a manger. Jesus's earthly mission began in Mary's womb. This is where the Holy Spirit formed and knitted His earthly body together. This is where God, the Son, took on our flesh. You see, He needed a mouth so that He could proclaim the good news to the poor. He needed shoulders so the government could rest upon them. He needed hands and feet so He could be nailed to the cross and save His people from their sins. He needed a brow so He could wear a crown of thorns. He needed a beating heart so that it could be stopped and He could die and defeat death. Jesus needed that body so He could be buried in a tomb and raised from the dead to the glory of the Father. It all began in Mary's womb. Jesus needed to be like us in every way, except without sin, not so that *He* could learn what it means to be human, but so *we* could learn what it means to be loved by the divine love of God! Jesus took on flesh for *your* sake. For to *you* is born a Savior, Jesus Christ, our Lord.

No one expected it to happen like that! No one expected a baby in a manger, a bloody cross, or an empty tomb. It was written in the law and the prophets, but no one could see it. Isn't that the way God works? He works in unexpected ways, like through this little church. (We're not much bigger than a manger!) Some of you didn't know what to expect when you came to worship here this evening. It's Christmas. *Expect Jesus.*

Wherever His Word is proclaimed, wherever believers gather in His name, He promises to be present, even this evening. Maybe you don't know what to expect tomorrow morning when you open your gifts, and that's a good thing. Because when you open that unexpected gift, the one that takes your breath away, that is merely a reflection of Jesus, the most unexpected gift of all. Born in a manger, died on a cross, and rose from the dead for *you* so that you can be saved from your sin and have eternal life with Him.

And just as Mary said when the angel announced Christ's birth, we say once again on this Christmas Eve: "May it be unto us according to Your Word, O Lord" (Luke 1:38). Will you bow your heads and pray with me?

"Our gracious, heavenly Father, hallow this night that it may be for us a holy night. Help us to hear your Holy Spirit speaking through your Word, that we may believe the good news of the gospel, that we may know your Son as our Savior—Jesus Christ, our Lord—and that we may be forgiven of our sins and receive eternal life. Open our hearts to hear the angels sing of your grace, and may we see your glory in Christ's birth. May His peace be for us. Amen."

Chapter 7

THE PRESENT

The year 2020—talk about the unexpected! As I look back over all my years in ministry—and over all my years on earth, for that matter—2020 was unprecedentedly unique. I've had some great years, some not-so-great years, years that brought great joys, and years that brought a little sadness. However, none of those years compare with 2020 and with experiencing the unexpected. At Trinity Lutheran Church, we spent the early part of 2020 strategically planning our fellowship and community events for the rest of the year, eager to get things rolling, and then came March. COVID-19 hit, and everything shut down. No fellowship events, no spring picnic, no karaoke nights, no game nights, no soup and Lenten Bible studies, no in-person services! What could we do?

As surprised and caught off guard as we were, Jesus wasn't either of those things. And through faith in Him, we continued doing ministry as His church. We found new ways to conduct worship (the drive-in style became very popular—and still is), we held holy communion services for ten or fewer communicants at a time, and we posted every service and bulletin online for our members who were worshiping "safe at home." In fact, the sermon you're about to encounter was held "drive-in style" on Christmas Eve in 2020. So, stay in your car, tune your radio to 1200 on your AM dial, and celebrate the birth of our Savior with us.

"The Present"—Christmas Eve, 2020

How many of you are ready for 2020 to be over? All I want for Christmas is a new year! It has been some kind of year, hasn't it? Obviously, with the virus, COVID-19 has affected almost everyone in some way, shape, or form.

We're out here in the parking lot this evening in response to safety protocols, social distancing, and so on. I see many of you wearing masks and repeatedly sanitizing your hands. My hands have never been so clean! In all seriousness, some folks have gotten extremely ill and are suffering with long-term effects from COVID, while others have lost their livelihoods because of shutdowns. Some of us have lost loved ones and good friends. The year 2020 has been a tough one, and not just here in this country, but across the world. 2021 cannot come fast enough! I think I'll give Ryan Seacrest a call and ask him to get the New Year's Eve party started early.

Please understand what I'm about to say. I don't want to be a party pooper or rain on our parade, but how do we know that 2021 will be any better than 2020? How do we know? It *could* be better. It could be worse. Think about 2020. Back in February, none of us saw what was coming. No one back in February thought that we'd be dealing with what we're dealing with right now! We couldn't see it. We couldn't predict it. So, why would we assume *anything* about 2021? We can hope!

We talked about the difference between faith and hope a few weeks ago; consequently, you understand that we can hope 2021 is better, but our faith is in God's Word that He will sustain us regardless of what happens. Here's our problem: we assume that we know more than we do, and we assume we can see more than we really can see. Listen to God's Word from James 4:13–15: "Come now, you who say, 'Today or tomorrow we will go into such and such a town and spend a year there and trade and make a profit.' [Next year's gonna be a lot better!] Yet you do not know what tomorrow will bring. What is your life? For you are a mist that appears for a little time and then vanishes. Instead, you ought to say, 'If the Lord wills, we will live and do this or that.'"

You do not know what tomorrow will bring. And you and I, we don't like *not knowing*. That makes us feel vulnerable. We don't like feeling vulnerable, so to not feel vulnerable, we make assumptions about what tomorrow will bring and disguise our assumptions as faith. But if we're honest, we do not know what tomorrow will bring.

At its very core, this is the essence of what makes us

human. Luther defined being human as creatures living in complete trust and dependence upon their Creator.[7] This applies to every single human being who has ever lived. Whether you believe in God or not, whether you're celebrating the birth of Christ or not, every single human being lives in complete dependence upon his and her Creator. Here's why: the air we breathe, we didn't manufacture that! The sun that gives us heat and life, we didn't create that. Our lives depend on those things. Imagine, in 2021, if the sun went supernova and disappeared from the sky. Imagine if all the oxygen in our atmosphere dissipated. That would be a lot worse than what happened in 2020! We live in complete dependence upon outside forces that we have nothing to do with and that we have no control over *whatsoever*. We live in complete dependence upon our Creator because we have no idea what tomorrow will bring. James says, "What is your life? For you are a mist that appears for a little time

---

[7] Robert Kolb, *Martin Luther and the Enduring Word of God: The Wittenberg School and Its Scripture-Centered Proclamation* (Grand Rapids: Baker Academic, 2016), 1–6, 8–10.

and then vanishes" (James 4:14). Not only do we not know what tomorrow will bring, but we can't say with certainty what the next ten minutes will bring. Some of you are hoping it will bring the end of this sermon!

In light of everything we just said, how are we to live right now, in this present moment? James also says, "You ought to say, 'If the Lord wills, we will live and do this or that'" (James 5:15). It's not a lack of faith to say, "If the Lord wills," but rather, it's the lack of assumption that says, "If the Lord wills." Complete dependence says, "If the Lord wills." Our Savior, God, the Son, in our flesh, Jesus Christ, our Lord, whose birth we're celebrating, He prayed, "Not my will, but yours, be done" (Luke 22:42). Complete dependence upon our heavenly Father: that's how we are to live right now in this present moment, because "we do not know what tomorrow will bring." This reminds me of some great words of wisdom from an ancient proverb that predates modern English: "Yesterday is history, tomorrow is a mystery, but today is a gift. That's why it is called the present." Today is all we have. Right now, this present moment is a gift from God. No one is guaranteed another moment in this life. Yes, we have eternal life through faith in Jesus, but in this life, in the here and now, this present moment is all we have. It is God's gift to you and me: to be here, gathered together and celebrating Christmas, hearing the good news of the gospel of Jesus. Your sins are forgiven, and through faith in Jesus, you are in right standing with God. This present moment: what a gift from God! That's the gift I'm asking God to give everyone I know and love. I pray that God enables you to live in the present, because in this life, that's all we have.

Sometime back in May or June, I had already thought about this Christmas Eve sermon. (I write down sermon ideas and text them to myself.) As bad as 2020 was going at that time, I thought to myself, *How can we make the best of this present moment?* I will say this: thanks be to God that a lot of good has come out of 2020. At home, in my family, we spent more time together. We had some great movie marathons! We also started and maintained a good workout routine. (I've lost twenty-five pounds, and I've kept it off!) At church, we've learned how to be flexible and to do worship a little differently. For Lutherans, that's a big deal! We now offer drive-in services all the time, during every service. That has really helped keep us together as a church family.

Understand, it's about making the most of the present moment because the present is a gift from God. We don't know what tomorrow will bring, but we do know what Jesus promises us in His Word. He will never leave us or forsake us. He is with us always, until the end of the age, which means He is with us right now, at this moment in time. Make the most of it! Love the people God has placed in your life at this moment. Hug your wife. Kiss your kids and grandkids. Pet the dog, for cryin' out loud!

In our family, we talk about our favorite days. "What's your favorite holiday?" Some of us like Thanksgiving, some like Halloween, and others like Christmas and Easter. Almost everybody likes his or her birthday (to a certain point!). Not too many of us like Mondays, and almost everybody likes Fridays. You know what my favorite day is? *Today.* Today is all I have. I don't know what tomorrow will bring. If the Lord wills, I will live and do this or that. But today, this evening, at this moment in time, I'm going to celebrate Christmas and the birth of Christ with the people I love and with the people God has placed in my life. What a gift from God: the present. And may it be unto us according to your Word, oh Lord. Amen.

P.S. Just as I was finishing this sermon during the 6:30 p.m. service on Christmas Eve, I heard a loud rumbling in the distance. As it got closer, the rumbling brought with it a monsoon-type rainstorm that blew our offering plates across the parking lot. It also blew over my pulpit that was set up on the front portico. Obviously, the drive-in service ended a little early that evening. I wasn't expecting that!

Chapter 8

FOREVER CHANGED

The next two chapters in this book are based on messages I presented on the fourth Sunday in Advent (the Sunday right before Christmas.) Chapter 8 focuses on how Joseph, Jesus's earthly father, dealt with the circumstances surrounding the birth of Christ, and chapter 9 focuses on how Mary dealt with those same circumstances. Grab a seat and join us as we hear the Word of the Lord and prepare our hearts for the upcoming celebration of our Savior's birth.

"Forever Changed"—The Fourth Sunday in Advent, 2017

One of the duties that comes with being a pastor is officiating wedding ceremonies. I enjoy weddings. It's an honor to be a part of people's lives in that way. It's an exciting time, and everyone is a little nervous. Even I'm a little nervous. I don't want any part of the ceremony to end up on *America's Funniest Home Videos*. It's my custom to meet with the couple before the wedding so I can get to know them a little better and find out their preferences for the ceremony. And then I sit back and listen to their story: how they met, what they have planned for their new life together, and where they see themselves in five years. Wedding bliss! They have no idea what's coming, do they? For anyone who has been married more than ten minutes, we know how life can change on a dime. Quite frankly, you don't need to be married to know that; you just need to be alive! In our gospel reading from Matthew 1, I bet Joseph and Mary had some great plans for their new life together, but then everything changed.

"Now the birth of Jesus Christ took place in this way. When his mother Mary had been betrothed to Joseph, before they came together, she was found to be with child" (Matthew 1:18). Houston, we have a problem. In plain English, you're not supposed to be found with child before the honeymoon. This threw a monkey wrench into Mary and Joseph's best-made plans for their new life together. Can you imagine Mary trying to explain to Joseph what was going on?

"Mary, how'd this happen? How'd you get pregnant?" Joseph asks.

Mary replies, "Joseph, it wasn't me! I promise! The angel Gabriel told me this was going to happen. I am with child from the Holy Spirit. This is God's Son."

Okay, what do they do now? So much for that honeymoon in the Keys. And forget about being upstanding members and running a successful family business in their community. Once folks got wind of this, their reputations would be ruined! What would they do then? In his gospel account, Matthew records that "Joseph, being a just man and unwilling to put her to shame, as he considered these things, he resolved to divorce her quietly" (Matthew 1:19). From Joseph's point of view, this was the best resolution and the best way for him to deal with the situation. All things being considered up to this point in narrative, it was more than fair. Legally, Joseph had the right to treat her much more harshly. But then everything changed again.

Continuing in Matthew 1:20–23, we read, "Behold, an angel of the Lord appeared to him in a dream, saying, 'Joseph, son of David, do not fear to take Mary as your wife, for that which is conceived in her is from the Holy Spirit. She will bear a son, and you shall call his name Jesus, for he will save his people from their sins.' All this took place to fulfill what the Lord had spoken by the prophet: 'Behold, the virgin shall conceive and bear a son, and they shall call his name Immanuel which means God with us.'"

In other words, Joseph, do not be afraid. Do not fear how this child will change your life. All this is taking place to fulfill what the Lord has already spoken. People may question, and people may scoff, ridicule you, and tell you how they would handle the situation if Mary was *their* wife! But do not resolve to do anything other than what the Lord commands you to do. His Word is now your final consideration. *His Son* is now your final consideration. Everything changed because of Jesus. Joseph and Mary's marital situation: their plans, their dreams, and their future together. Jesus changed everything, and Joseph was afraid. Mary was also afraid; that's why in Luke 1:30, the angel Gabriel told Mary, "Do not be afraid!"

You see, the very thing they were afraid of, Mary being found with child (and not just any child, but the Son of God), was the very thing that would bring salvation not only to them, but to all of us. Jesus, Immanuel, God with us: "He will save his people from their sins." So how did Joseph deal with change? How did Joseph deal with his entire life being turned upside down? Listen to Mathew 1:24: "When Joseph woke from sleep, he did as the angel of the Lord commanded him." What

Joseph resolved to do, to divorce Mary quietly, fell by the wayside. His considerations, his resolutions, and his fears were forever changed by the Word of the Lord and by the Word of the Lord made flesh, Jesus Christ.

How do you deal with change? How do you deal with things not going according to your best-made plans? Like those newlyweds we talked about a moment ago, we all have ideas about the way we think things are supposed to happen. We all assume that *we know* the way things are supposed to happen. But when circumstances throw a monkey wrench into our plans and our lives are turned upside down, what do we do? We tend to get bent out of shape because we live under the false assumption that we know our futures and that we're in control of what's going to happen. The world tells us we're supposed to be in control. Self-help gurus teach us that we're in control. Some Christians even teach the same thing. If you have enough faith, or if you do enough good deeds (i.e., if you're not on the naughty list), then you can control what happens. Really? Give me a chapter and a verse in the Bible for that.

Like I've said in previous sermons, the only thing we can control is how we respond to circumstances. Like Joseph and Mary—and every other human being, for that matter—it all comes down to this: change exposes the fact that we're not in control. Therefore, we're afraid of change because it exposes our vulnerabilities. So, we fight for control. But fighting for control means fighting against God. Guess who wins that fight? Obviously, God does. God is in control. And the sooner you and I get ahold of that truth, the sooner we'll be able to deal with the ever-changing circumstances in our lives. Here's the best news you'll hear all day: If you're baptized and believe in Jesus, then you have no need to fight for control. Everything forever changed in your life the moment you were baptized into Christ. I'll give you a chapter and verse for that.

In Romans 6:3–4, the apostle Paul writes, "Do you not know that all of us who have been baptized into Christ Jesus were baptized into his death? We were buried therefore with him by baptism into death, in order that just as Christ was raised from the dead by the glory of the Father, we too might walk in newness of life." Everything changed in your life when you were united with Christ in the waters of your baptism. That may be a hard pill to swallow, especially for us die-hard Lutherans. You've heard the jokes about how Lutherans resist change, right? "How many Lutherans does it take to change a light bulb? None, because we still use candles!"

I like to tell people, "Lutherans love change. Look at our offerings!" We need not fear change. We need not fear how being united with Jesus changes our lives. We're in a continual state of change, always living and learning and growing through our faith in Christ. As a result, we know that He has a purpose for every circumstance that has or that will ever affect our lives. I have chapters and verses for that too: Romans 8:28: "All things work together for good, for those who are called according to his purpose." James 1:2: "Count it all joy when you fall into various trials, knowing that the testing of your faith produces patience." People may question you; people may scoff at you and ridicule you and tell you how they would handle things if they were in your situation. But here's the deal: don't resolve to do anything other than what the Lord commands you to do. Like Joseph, His Word is now your final consideration. His Son is now your final consideration.

We are not our own; we belong to Jesus, and we were bought with a price. That's the best news you'll hear all day! What the angel said to Joseph, Jesus whispers to us as His baptized children. *Do not fear what may happen in your life. All things are taking place to fulfill my purpose.* The very thing we fear, change, is the very thing the Lord uses to strengthen our faith, to wake us up, and to keep our hearts focused. We *are* vulnerable and weak, and apart from Jesus, we can do nothing. However, we are not our own anymore. Now our lives serve a greater purpose. Everything forever changed when Jesus purchased us with His blood and united us in baptism.

A Rhetorical Question

Why should we pray? If Jesus is in control and works all things for our good, then why should we pray? I offer the prayer list we pray over during our worship services as an answer. We have a lot of people on our prayer list with all kinds of ailments and issues, and we pray for these people. We pray for healing, for God to provide, and for God to strengthen and protect. I have no idea what tomorrow holds for any of them. But I do know that Jesus told us to pray for one another, and together we pray as our Lord taught us. Now, within the Lord's Prayer there is a statement, "Thy Kingdom come. Thy will be done on earth as it is in heaven" (Matthew 6:10). Thy will, not my will.

The Lord hears and answers our prayers, and yet He works all things together for good according to His will and purpose. All things include *how* he answers our prayers. I don't know *God's* will in every situation, but I do know what *I* will. I know what I believe is good, right, and salutary. I want God to heal, to deliver, and to provide. But it's not always about what I want or what you want. It's about the greater purpose that our lives now serve. What if God is using our hardships to teach others how to remain faithful when they go through the same thing? Paul says in 2 Corinthians 1:3–4, "Praise be to the God and Father of our Lord Jesus Christ, who comforts us in all our troubles, so that we can comfort those with the comfort we ourselves have received from God."

What if everything I went through up to this point in my life is for the benefit of my children? Maybe they're the ones who are going to change the world. I'm just planting a seed. "Neither he who plants nor he who waters is anything, but only God who gives the growth" (1 Corinthians 3:5). It's not always about what you or I can see, understand, and perceive. It goes far beyond our perceptions. Maybe the trials and hardships you're going through aren't just about you. Your children are watching. Your grandchildren are watching. Your friends are watching.

Maybe God desires to show Christ to them through

your faithfulness. You and I are baptized into Christ, and our lives are not our own. Don't be afraid of that. Don't be afraid to be vulnerable and weak. Don't be afraid of change. The only thing that never changes is the one we're trusting: Jesus, the one we're looking to for all good and help in the midst of our continual change. Jesus Christ is the same yesterday, today, and forever. He is in control, and you and I belong to Him. And may it be unto us according to His Word. Amen.

Chapter 9

LET IT BE UNTO US

Almost every year at Trinity, we participate in some type of yearly Bible reading plan. We've read through the Bible in one year and in two years, and we've read through the Bible chronologically. At the time of this writing, we're reading through the New Testament, along with the books of Proverbs and Psalms in one year (which is only about one chapter per day.) I normally send email reminders at the beginning of the week to the members on our email list so we can read through the Bible together as a church family. What type of Bible reading plan we use during any given year is not the emphasis; the emphasis is on making a commitment as God's people to read His Word. Everything we do as a church and as individual believers revolves around and is centered upon the Word of God. And as you're about to hear in the sermon, reading the Bible is not an end unto itself. There is a purpose for reading the scriptures. So grab your Bible, turn to the gospel of Luke 1:28–38, and hear God's Word for the fourth Sunday in Advent, 2020.

"Let It Be Unto Us …"—The Fourth Sunday in Advent, 2020

Why do you read the Bible? What are your reasons for reading it? Maybe you turn to the Bible for insight. It does provide insight into many of life's tough questions, but it is more than just insightful. Maybe you turn to the Bible for inspiration. It does provide inspiration, but it's more than just inspirational. Maybe you read the Bible only when you feel guilty about not reading the Bible. You read it out of duty because you know you're supposed to. Here's the point: *why* we read the Bible directly influences *how* we read the Bible. If we turn to the Bible just to gather information or to gain insight, then we read it like an encyclopedia or a dictionary. In doing so, we overlook the purpose of God's Word, and we miss so much of what God's Word is doing to us. Even though the Bible is full of great information and is highly inspirational, the Bible's purpose is *transformation*. The Bible is God's Word to you and me, and God transforms us as He personally speaks to us through His Word. We're not saved by information, insight, inspiration, or dutiful devotion. We're saved by God personally transforming us into a people who have faith in Jesus. This is the work of the Holy Spirit, and He does that through the Word.

When we read the Bible, it's really the Holy Spirit reading us. When we open the book, it's really the Holy Spirit opening us. Look at Hebrews 4:12–13: "For the word of God is living and active, sharper than any two-edged sword, piercing to the division of soul and of spirit, of joints and of marrow, and discerning the thoughts and intentions of the heart." The Bible is God's activity. It's alive; it pierces, divides, discerns, and creates. In one of my favorite quotes from Luther, he says, "For God to speak is the same as to do, for His Word is the deed."[8] Since God does all this through His Word, why should we read the Bible? Because God transforms us as He speaks to us. How should we read the Bible? We should *hear* it. We should hear what God is saying and then discern what He's speaking to us through His Word. Rather than reading it like any old book, we should learn to hear what God speaks just like when we listen to a sermon. We're to hear His voice in scripture. Our text for this week's sermon is a great example of God transforming someone through His Word.

> An Angel came to Mary and said, "Greetings, O favored one, the Lord is with you!" Mary was greatly troubled at the saying and tried to discern what sort of greeting this might be. And the angel said to her, "Do not be afraid, Mary, for God has given you unmerited favor. And

---

[8] Martin Luther, "Psalm 2," in *Luther's Works*, eds. E. Theodore Bachmann and Helmut T. Lehmann (Philadelphia: Fortress Press, 1971), vol. 12, 33.

behold, you will conceive in your womb and bear a son, and you shall call his name Jesus. He will be great and will be called the Son of the Most High. And the Lord God will give to him the throne of his father David, and he will reign over the house of Jacob forever, and of his kingdom there will be no end." And Mary said to the angel, "How will this be, since I am a virgin?" (Luke 1:28–34)

When God's Word came to Mary through the angel Gabriel, Mary was greatly troubled; *she was afraid.* Her mind had to be racing with all kinds with questions. Practically speaking, what were the implications? Mary was betrothed to Joseph, and a betrothal usually preceded marriage by at least nine months to assure that the bride wasn't pregnant. Mary's pregnancy was going to show well before that nine-month timeline was up. How would she defend herself against the slander? The accusations? Who was going to believe her story? How would she overcome the naysayers and the suspicions? And not just that; this was God's Son she was bringing into the world. Think about this: Mary was well aware of how her people, Israel, treated the prophets. They rejected and killed them. Now, she was bringing God's own Son to them! How could she protect her little baby from the forces that would come against Him? They might reject and kill Him, just as they did the prophets. She would certainly need the fullest protection from God to bring Jesus into this world.

Mary was afraid, and she had real questions. Fear and human reasoning do not mix well with God's unmerited favor. However, God anticipated Mary's questions, and through His messenger, God spoke His Word to her to calm her fears. "The Lord is with you!" and "Do not be afraid." and "God has given you unmerited favor" (with both God and humanity). The assurance of the Lord's protection and favor was given to her at that very moment. If you remember the rest of story, God granted her great favor with Joseph (through a dream); God protected them from Herod; and the Bible records that, as Jesus grew up and become strong, the favor of God was upon Him.

I want you think about how often God speaks words of unmerited favor to you. God's unmerited favor is simply this: the promises of the gospel spoken over you. Whether it's spoken through the biblical writers as you read and hear God's promises, or whether it's spoken through a pastor in a sermon or in the sacraments or in a hymn or a spiritual song, God speaks unmerited favor to you every time you hear, "The Lord is with you! Your sins are forgiven."

Every time you hear the benediction, "The Lord bless you and keep you," that's a promise of the gospel! That's God's unmerited favor spoken over you! But there are times when we don't feel like the Lord is with us and we don't sense His favor. Fear and human reasoning often ring louder in our ears than God's Word. Like Mary, we have some of the same questions troubling us. God gave you and me unmerited favor? Why? What are the implications? Realize that, along with God's favor comes a calling to be His ambassadors on this earth and disciples of Christ. This calling is monumental. Look at the world around us. How can we even begin to make a difference? Our situation is not unlike Mary's, although on a much smaller scale. We're not birthing Christ into the world, but we are *bringing* Christ to the world. God speaks His Word to us, and our initial responses are usually, "Why'd ya pick me? How's this going to work? Who will believe me?" Listen to Gabriel's response to Mary's questions, and by extension, to our questions as well.

Luke 1:35–38: "And Gabriel answered her, 'The Holy Spirit, the power of the Most High, will overshadow you; therefore the child to be born will be called holy— the Son of God. And behold, your relative, Elizabeth, in her old age has also conceived a son, and this is the sixth month with her who was called barren. For nothing will be impossible with God.' And Mary said, 'Behold, I am the servant of the Lord; let it be to me according to your word.'"

What a passage of scripture! How is this going to work? *Nothing will be impossible with God.* Who will believe me? *Nothing will be impossible with God.* Did you hear Mary's response, the second time around? "Behold, I am the servant of the Lord. Let it be to me according to your word." Fear and human reasoning were transformed into trust and faithfulness when God's unmerited favor was spoken to her. She was transformed through hearing God's Word. "For God to speak is the same as to do, for His Word is the deed."

In this passage, there are two observations that I want to touch on—brief asides, if you will. First, think about the contrast between Eve and Mary. In the garden, Eve rejected God's Word, and through her and Adam's actions, brought sin and death upon us all. That was when God made the promise in Genesis 3:15 that one day, the seed of the woman would crush the head of the serpent. Now we come to Mary, the woman Genesis 3:15 is referring to. When God spoke unmerited favor to her, she believed God's Word. In essence, Mary is the antithesis of Eve, and through the power of the Holy Spirit, Jesus, the promised seed, was born in the flesh and brought salvation upon us all. Now, instead of sin and death reigning, forgiveness and eternal life reigns through faith in Jesus, the promised seed of the woman Mary.

The second observation is that when the angel told Mary "nothing will be impossible with God" (Luke 1:37), does that remind you of anything else in scripture? Do you remember the words of Jesus when the disciples asked Him, "Then who can be saved?" (Matthew 10:26). Jesus looked at them and answered, "With man it is impossible, but not with God. For all things are possible with God" (Matthew 10:27).

Human reason can't figure out why God would come into this world to save us. It's God's unmerited favor. It's grace! We have nothing to do with it. We don't choose it. We can't buy it. It's simply spoken to us. Unmerited favor: God gave it to Mary, and God gives it to us today through His Word. Whether it's God's Word in creation, God's Word incarnate, or God's Word in the sermon and sacraments, "For God to speak is the same as to do, for His Word is the deed."

Why does God speak unmerited favor to us?

Transformation. God transforms us so that we'll trust in Jesus. That's what this passage in Luke is all about. It's not about glorifying Mary; she knew she was just the servant of the Lord. It's not about glorifying the angel; he knew he was just a messenger of the Lord. It's not about glorifying ourselves; we're just recipients of God's unmerited favor. It's about God transforming us into people who have faith and trust in Jesus for salvation. Like Mary, God's Spirit hovers over us as God speaks His Word and faith in Jesus is born in our hearts.

This is basically the same process Luther describes in his explanation of the third article of the creed. "I believe that I cannot by my own reason or strength believe in Jesus Christ my Lord or come to Him, but the Holy Spirit has called me by the gospel, enlightened me with His gifts, sanctified, and kept me in the true faith."[9] Again, we hear it in Article V of the Augsburg Confession, "The ministry of preaching the gospel and

---

[9] Robert Kolb and Timothy J. Wengert, eds. *The Book of Concord: The Confessions of the Evangelical Lutheran Church* (Minneapolis: Fortress Press, 2000), 355.

administering the sacraments was instituted by Christ for this purpose,"[10] the purpose of transformation. Nothing will be impossible with God, and Mary's response right after the angel said that was, "Behold, I am the servant of the Lord, let it be to me according to your Word." (Luke 1:38).

Think about all the impossibilities that were made possible after Mary had this conversation with Gabriel. First, Joseph believed her (after he was convinced by a dream). When Jesus grew up, He turned water into wine. He healed the sick, raised the dead, calmed the storm, and walked on water. And then He was crucified right in front of Mary, his own mother! And on the third day, He rose from the dead. Nothing will be impossible with God. With man it is impossible, but not with God. For all things are possible with God. I'm sure none of this happened the way Mary envisioned it would when the angel spoke those words to her before the birth of

---

[10] Robert Kolb and Timothy J. Wengert, eds. *The Book of Concord: The Confessions of the Evangelical Lutheran Church* (Minneapolis: Fortress Press, 2000), 41.

Christ. But God still did the impossible through Christ. And please understand what I'm about to say: in this sermon, you're hearing the same words that Mary heard. This is just as much God's Word now as when it was spoken by the angel! I'm telling each one of you, nothing will be impossible with God.

I want you to think about all those impossible things you're praying about, those gut-wrenching, heartbreaking, keep-you-awake-at-night things: nothing will be impossible with God. His answer to your prayers may not be what you envisioned, but do not be afraid, for God has given you unmerited favor in Christ! And the Holy Spirit, the power of the Most High, overshadows you. Therefore, nothing will be impossible with God. Do you believe that? Do you really believe that? Mary believed it as much as a person can believe when God tells them something like that. She obviously didn't know all the details, and she couldn't see the future, but she trusted and that's why she responded, *let it be to me according to your Word*. Her fear and her reasoning were silenced by God's Word, and she was transformed.

I imagine, like Mary, we believe. And even though we don't know the details and cannot see the future, we will trust God; His Word will silence our fears and our human reasoning, and we will be transformed. And just as we do after almost every sermon, we echo Mary's response, "Let it be unto us according to your Word. Amen."

Chapter 10

CELEBRATE JESUS

This final chapter contains the message I delivered on Christmas morning in 2016. At Trinity Lutheran Church, our custom is not to hold worship services on Christmas Day unless it falls on a Sunday. Parishioners have asked me why this is, and I've answered that, "We celebrate Christ's birth together as a church family on Christmas Eve. On Christmas Day, I celebrate Christ's birth with my wife and kids." More succinctly, I dedicate Christmas Eve to my church family, and Christmas Day is dedicated to my immediate family. On Christmas Day, my God-given vocation as husband to my wife and father to my children takes precedent over my God-given vocation as pastor. However, this particular Christmas

Day fell on a Sunday, so I fulfilled the duties of both vocations to church and to family. My wife and I, along with our children, woke up extra early that morning and opened our Christmas gifts, and then off we went to the 10:00 a.m. worship service. Now that we're all here, I hope you're awake and that you've had plenty of coffee, because it's time to celebrate!

"Celebrate Jesus"—Christmas Day, 2016

As many of you are aware, I'm not a morning person! Some people wake up and say, "Good morning, Lord!" I'm one of those people who wakes up and grumbles, "Good Lord, it's morning." The first folks to arrive at church early in the morning before service can attest to this. They take one look at me and ask, "Are you awake yet?" They usually find me in the cry room sitting in a rocking chair, having some quiet time. If I don't answer, it's only because their voices don't register in my ears that early in the morning. It's kind of like Charlie Brown in the classroom when the teacher is talking: "Whaaa,

whaaa, whaaa." All I hear in the morning is, "Whaaa, whaaa, whaaa."

By the way, this may come as a shock, but I quit drinking coffee—or should I say, I cut caffeine out my diet for the most part. I still drink decaf coffee and decaf sodas. It hasn't affected my mornings so much, but I do feel better in the afternoons. I'm not crashing from a caffeine high anymore. Needless to say, mornings are still a challenge for me. However, there are a few exceptions. I do like Sunday mornings, once I'm up and at 'em! I enjoy the opportunity of worshipping with all you fine people. The other exception is Christmas morning. I love Christmas morning. So, this morning is a double whammy!

For me, and for most of you, Christmas morning, Sunday mornings, and Saturday nights at Trinity Lutheran Church all have something in common. This is when we set aside time specifically to celebrate Jesus—to celebrate His birth, His life, His death, His resurrection, and to receive His gifts to us. In our text for today, I want you to *hear* why Jesus is worthy of our celebration. I want you to *hear* what the Bible reveals about our Savior.

Hebrews 1:1–3 says, "Long ago, at many times and in many ways, God spoke to our fathers by the prophets, but in these last days he has spoken to us by His Son, whom He appointed the heir of all things, through whom also He created the world. He is the radiance of the glory of God and the exact imprint of His nature, and He upholds the universe by the word of His power. After making purification for sins, He sat down at the right hand of the majesty on high …" These first three verses in Hebrews lay the foundation for what the author presents in the remainder of his letter. The author is making a plea to Jewish Christians who were suffering intense persecution at the hand of Rome. Christianity was illegal, but Judaism was not. So, in his letter, he encourages Christians to keep the faith in Jesus because regardless of the legal status, *regardless of persecution,* there is no turning back to Judaism. Jesus made that clear. Everything in the Old Testament foreshadows and points forward to Jesus, and faith in Jesus is the only way to continue to faithfully serve God. To those who claimed that they could serve God by following Moses's teaching, Jesus said, "If you believed Moses, you would believe me, for he wrote of me" (John 5:46). To those who claimed that they could serve God because they were Abraham's descendants, Jesus said, "Abraham rejoiced that he would see my day, he saw it and was glad. Truly, truly, I say to you, before Abraham was, I am!" (John 8:56, 58). Remember, they were going to kill Jesus for saying that He was the great I am, the God of the Old Testament. And finally, Jesus said, "If God were really your Father [if that's who you're really serving], then you would know Me. I and my Father are one" (John 10:30). Jesus makes it all too clear: He is both the purpose and the fulfillment of every word spoken in the Old Testament and in the Bible. Jesus is God's Word made flesh.

In John 5:39–40, Jesus said, "You search the scriptures because you think that in them you have eternal life: it is they that bear witness about me, yet you refuse to come to me that you may have life." This reminds me of one of my Old Testament professors at seminary. He said when you study, read, or preach from the Old Testament, eventually, "You've got to get to Jesus!" The author of Hebrews repeats this same point over and over in his letter. Jesus is greater than Moses. Jesus is greater than the angels. Jesus is the great high priest. Through His death and resurrection, Jesus fulfills and completes the temple sacrificial system. The blood of Jesus establishes a new and greater covenant. Again, there's nothing left for the Jewish people to turn back to because Jesus is both the continuation and fulfillment of Judaism, and Jesus is the only way to know God. Hence, the author of Hebrews begins his letter with a fascinating testimony about who Jesus is. This is what we will focus on in the remainder of this morning's Christmas message. This may feel kind of like a Bible study, but I figured that would be okay, as long as we get to Jesus!

Hebrews 1:1 says, "Long ago, at many times and in many ways, God spoke to our fathers by the prophets ..." Literally, in many parts and in many portions over a vast period of time. For example, God spoke some things to Abraham; God spoke some things to Isaac, Jacob, Joseph, Moses, the major and minor prophets, and so on.

Hebrews 1:2 says, "But in these last days He has spoken to us by His Son, whom He appointed the heir of all things, through whom also He created the world." In this verse, the author describes three activities that God, the Father, accomplishes through God, the Son. First, "In these last days He has spoken to us by His Son." Something has changed in these last days: what God is saying through His Son is His final word to humankind. There's nothing more that God needs to say. God took on our flesh, and in Christ, God speaks to humanity face to face! Furthermore, Jesus fulfills all that God has ever spoken previously, at many times and in many ways through the Old Testament saints, prophets, and priests. Second, God appointed Jesus "the heir of all things." All that was lost because of our fall into sin, Jesus reclaims for us. Now, we can be forgiven of our sins and have a right relationship with God. Now, we can have eternal life. Christ now restores everything that Adam lost in the fall, and He gives all these things back to those who believe and have faith in Him. And third, "Through whom [speaking of Jesus] God created the World." God, the Son, wasn't created; He always existed with the Father and the Holy Spirit. Everything that was created—time, energy, space, matter—was created through Jesus Christ. God spoke, appointed, and created all things through the Son. This leads us to the next verse.

In Hebrews 1:3, the author describes several attributes of the Son: "He is the radiance of the glory of God." Jesus doesn't reflect God's radiance and glory: He is God's radiance and glory because He is "the exact imprint of God's nature." Jesus is the exact expression of the Father in heaven. Jesus is the only way to see, hear, and know who God is. According to our understanding of the Trinity, the Father and the Son are two distinct persons but they, along with the Holy Spirit, are undivided according to their substance. Another attribute of the Son in verse three is the fact that Jesus "upholds the universe by the word of His power." In other words, the time, energy, space, and matter that was created through

Jesus Christ is also sustained and continues moving forward through Jesus Christ. What the author is telling us here is that Jesus is the foundation for our existence. He is how we understand who God is and who we're supposed to be within God's creation. Literally, Jesus is Creator and creation brought together in one person! Jesus is true God and true human, and He knows how to bring God and humanity together because that is who He is. That's why, when Jesus did the things that He did during his earthly ministry, he blew the disciples' minds! When Jesus healed the sick, raised the dead, and calmed the storm, it wasn't miraculous to Him. It wasn't magic; it was just the work of the Creator doing what He does. Jesus created the time, energy, and space-matter continuum in which we now exist, and He knows how to manipulate it, how to fix it, and how to fix us. In the last part of verse three, the author of Hebrews reveals how Jesus fixes us, along with all of humanity.

Hebrews 1:3 continues by stating that "after making purification for sins …" we're forgiven and free because Jesus forgives and frees us from the power of sin. As we hear all these amazing details about Jesus, hopefully we understand why He alone is qualified to forgive us of our sins. Jesus is God: God with us and God for us. After all this, the author of Hebrews concludes verse three by saying that he "sat down at the right hand of the majesty on High." This is a significant statement, and here's why: There wasn't a chair in the Old Testament temple because the work of the priest was never finished. In Hebrews 10:11–14, the author says, "Every priest *stands* daily at his service, offering repeatedly the same sacrifices, which can never take away sins. But when Christ had offered for all time a single sacrifice for sins, He *sat down* at the right hand of God … For by a single offering Jesus perfected for all time those who are being sanctified." On the cross Jesus said, "It is finished" (John 19:30). Jesus's work of saving us from our sins and His work of fixing us and all of creation is *finished*.

And here's the kicker: all this divine activity, God speaking, God appointing, and God creating, as well as these divine attributes—God's radiance, God's nature, God's power and forgiveness—all of it was wrapped in swaddling clothes and lying in a manger. The fullness of God was lying in a trough used to feed animals! The babe born in a manger is God Almighty. No wonder we celebrate Christmas. No wonder we celebrate Jesus. This is such a special time of year. I'm not in a hurry to take down the Christmas tree. I'm not in a hurry to take down the decorations, though I'm glad the shopping's over! And the truth is, every Sunday throughout the year, we'll continue to celebrate Christmas and continue to celebrate Jesus. From the cradle to the cross, from the cross to the empty tomb, from His ascension to the season of Pentecost, the entire church year celebrates Jesus. The celebration may not always include lights and presents, but through listening to and hearing Jesus's words, and through receiving the sacraments that He instituted, we celebrate Jesus. We celebrate who He is and what He has accomplished for us. We're going to do that all year long, even if it means getting up early to celebrate. I don't need coffee to do that, but I may need a little quiet time in the cry room before service! And may it be unto us according to your Word. Amen.